UNSUNG HEROES
of Hispanic Heritage

SYLVIA MENDEZ

A PIONEER FOR EQUALITY IN EDUCATION

Tammy Gagne

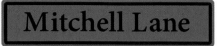

PUBLISHERS

2001 SW 31st Avenue
Hallandale, FL 33009
www.mitchelllane.com

First Edition, 2021.
Author: Tammy Gagne
Designer: Ed Morgan
Editor: Morgan Brody

Series: Unsung Heroes of Hispanic Heritage
Title: Sylvia Mendez: A Pioneer for Equality in Education / by Tammy Gagne

Hallandale, FL : Mitchell Lane Publishers, [2021]

Library bound ISBN: 978-1-68020-679-1
eBook ISBN: 978-1-68020-680-7

CONTENTS

CHAPTER ONE

1

BREAKING DOWN BARRIERS

"Congratulations, my sweet Sofia!"

"Thank you, Abuela," Sofia said as she hugged her beloved grandmother. The eighth-grade graduation ceremony had just ended. Sofia's family now gathered outside the middle school to take photos and celebrate with her.

"Have you chosen any of your classes yet for fall?" her grandmother asked. Like everyone else, Abuela assumed that Sofia would be attending the public high school just down the road. But Sofia had other plans.

"Actually," she announced, "I have applied to Hayden's school." She took a deep breath and let it out. It felt good to finally tell everyone. She had no idea how her parents would respond to this news. Hayden was Sofia's older brother. The school he attended was ranked among the best high schools in their state. It also had a strict boys-only admittance policy.

"Good for you, sis," Hayden said and raised his hand for a high five. Hayden knew his younger sister could do anything she set her mind to accomplishing. Her grades were even better than his, and he was an excellent student. Her parents stood with their mouths open. They clearly hadn't expected this development.

Before anyone could remind her of her odds of getting into the school, Sofia added, "I've already received my first rejection letter. I realize that getting in won't be easy. I just think that it's wrong to refuse to admit students on the basis of their gender. I'm ready to fight this policy, and I would like your help."

"You remind me of Sylvia Mendez," Abuela said. "Do you know who that is?"

In the 1940s, Mexican American children did not receive the same education as other American kids.

"I sure do," Sofia replied with a smile. "In 1946, a California school turned her away because it only accepted white students," she told the rest of her family. "Sylvia's father was an immigrant from Mexico. Her mother had come here from Puerto Rico like Abuela. They helped Sylvia fight for the right to the same education that white students could receive."

Brown v. Board of Education remains an important ruling in U.S. history. Many families whose parents or grandparents came to the United States as immigrants teach their children about the Supreme Court case.

"That's right," her grandmother said. She was obviously proud that Sofia already knew the story. Most people knew about *Brown v. Board of Education*. This 1954 U.S. Supreme Court case ruled that separating students by race was unconstitutional. What many people didn't know is that the Mendez court case in Los Angeles was a stepping-stone to that important ruling. The Mendez family broke down barriers for other minority students in the United States.

"We will help you in any way we can," Sofia's father responded. She couldn't help but notice a tear in his eye. He turned to his son. "I'm so proud of all the hard work you put into school, Hayden. Now it's time to help your sister get that same opportunity."

REFUSED FOR RACE

Sylvia Mendez was in the third grade when the 17th Street Elementary School in Westminster, California refused to admit her because she was Mexican American.

CHAPTER TWO

RAISING THEIR VOICES

Sylvia Mendez is seen here with her sister Sandra and her brother Gonzalo, Jr. beside a photograph of their parents.

Sylvia Mendez was born on June 7, 1936, in Santa Ana, California. Her parents, Gonzalo and Felicitas Mendez, had come to the United States from Mexico because they dreamed of a bright future for their family. They had heard that people willing to work hard could make their dreams come true in the United States. Because of their courage to make a new life in their neighboring country, little Sylvia would one day be able to make her own dreams a reality.

Sylvia was a lot like other little girls her age. She enjoyed learning new things from her teacher. She also liked playing with her friends at recess. But her elementary school was different from the schools many other kids attended. The Mendez family had moved to Westminster during World War II. White children who lived in this city went to a well-kept school. The government forced Sylvia and the other Mexican American children in her neighborhood to attend a separate school. The only reason for this separation was that they were of Mexican descent.

Sylvia's school was in horrible shape. It consisted of a shoddy building. Instead of a fun playground, it had a dirt yard. There were no swings or monkey bars like the other school had. An electric fence circled the area, which was next to a cow pasture. This dreary, dangerous space was far from the dream that Sylvia's parents had imagined for their children. When they tried to enroll Sylvia in the nicer school, they were told Mexican children could not attend. The Mendez family decided to sue the school district so Mexican American kids could go to the nicer school, too.

Sylvia attended the Hoover School. The building on the left was for the lower grades like Sylvia, while the older children used the building on the right.

In the beginning nine-year-old Sylvia did not understand just how much she was being denied. Years later, she told a writer from *Teen Vogue*, "I was seeing this beautiful [white] school, large concrete courtyard, a beautiful playground . . . I thought 'I know what they're fighting for. They're fighting so I can go to that beautiful school and have a playground.'"

This was indeed part of what her parents were seeking for their young daughter. But they were also fighting for something much bigger. They wanted all Mexican American children to get the same education as the white children. Keeping people separated due to race is called segregation. The Mendez family thought segregation was wrong. They knew the only way they might stop it was by challenging the law. Three other families joined in the Mendez's lawsuit. Together they fought against segregation in four school districts in Southern California.

Frank Palomino joined the Mendez family in their lawsuit against the school district. He wanted his sons, Arthur (*3rd row, 2nd from left*) and Bobby (*back row, right*), to be able to get the same education as white children received. The boys attended fourth grade at the Fremont School.

OPENING DOORS FOR OTHERS

Although the *Mendez v. Westminster* lawsuit involved just four families, they were fighting for the rights of 5,000 Mexican American students. If they won, these kids would also be able to attend schools with "whites-only" policies.

Spanish American children were just as smart and willing to learn as their white counterparts in the 1940s. They just needed the same opportunities.

CHAPTER THREE

CHANGING THE WORLD

David Marcus

A lawyer named David Marcus represented Sylvia's family in the court case. In order to win, Marcus needed to convince the judge that Sylvia and the other Mexican American students would suffer from being segregated. People who believed that segregation was fair often insisted that it made things separate but equal. The Mexican American families knew better. The run-down buildings and sparse play spaces were just the most obvious ways their kids were being treated unfairly. Their children also faced a very real but less visible disadvantage.

Marcus argued that being taught separately was bad for the self-esteem of the Mexican American children. He researched the ways that segregation affected how students saw themselves. He explained to the judge that when Mexican American kids were not allowed to attend the same schools as white children, they began to feel like they were not as good as the white children. Marcus also pointed out that these feelings would likely keep the Mexican American students from succeeding in both school and later life.

On March 18, 1946, U.S. District Court Judge Paul J. McCormick ruled in favor of Mendez and the other families who joined the lawsuit. He wrote in his decision that social equality was vital to education. "It must be open to all children by unified school association regardless of lineage," he stated.

U.S. District Court Judge Paul J. McCormick changed the futures for numerous Mexican American children with his ruling in the Mendez case.

CHAPTER **THREE**

McCormick's ruling was a huge victory for the students and their families. But the fight was far from over. The school districts appealed the decision. This means that they wanted a higher court to consider the case. If that court came to a different decision, its ruling would cancel out the first decision. The law is often a complicated matter. Many court cases get caught up in appeals for many months or even years. Some even make it all the way to the U.S. Supreme Court. This is the highest court in the country. The U.S. Court of Appeals for the 9th Circuit made the final ruling in the *Mendez v. Westminster* case on April 14, 1947. It held up Judge McCormick's ruling.

The U.S. Supreme Court building in
Washingon D.C.

Still, many other U.S. school districts clung to segregation. One of them was in Kansas. In 1951, an all-white school in Topeka denied admittance to an African American girl named Linda Brown. Like Sylvia's parents, Linda's father decided to sue the school system. This case, which reached the U.S. Supreme Court, made segregation illegal throughout the United States. Without the Mendez verdict, though, this might never have happened. Brown's lawyer, Thurgood Marshall, used the Mendez case as an important example in court. Although Sylvia's case had ended seven years earlier, it played an important part in ending segregation for good.

This photograph taken at the Barnard School in Washington, D.C. in 1955 might have looked much different had it not been for the courage of Sylvia Mendez's family.

A STATE-WIDE CHANGE

Two months after the Court of Appeals ruled, California Governor Earl Warren signed a new bill into state law. It made segregation illegal in all California public schools.

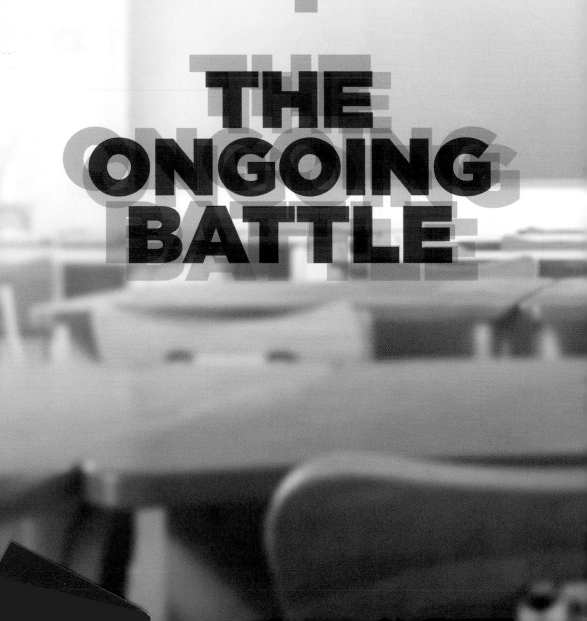

CHAPTER FOUR

4

THE
ONGOING
BATTLE

Sylvia Mendez was excited to attend the 17th Street Elementary School in Westminster. She looked forward to studying new topics and making new friends there. She pictured playing with them on the playground. What she did not expect was the bullying she faced. Some people dislike other people for no reason other than their race. This is called racism. Some of the kids picked on the Mexican American children who joined the student body after Sylvia's court case. During an interview with StoryCorps, Sylvia recalled one white boy at the school who confronted her on the playground. "This little white boy comes up and he says, 'What are you doing here? You don't belong in this school. They shouldn't have Mexicans here.'"

The boy told her to go back to Mexico. He did not understand that Sylvia had been born in the United States, that she was as much a U.S. citizen as he was.

Taunts like this one from other students made Sylvia feel sad and unwelcome. One day she came home in tears because of the bullying. She told her mother that she didn't ever want to go back to the school. But Felicitas reminded her daughter that she had a right to attend this school. The family had fought long and hard for it. Now it was time to finish the hard work that they had begun by getting the education she deserved. After a good night's sleep, Sylvia returned to school the next day.

She remained dedicated to her studies long after she left the 17th Street School. After high school, she enrolled in Orange Coast Community College. There, she earned an Associate's Degree in Nursing. Later, she graduated from California State University with a bachelor's degree in the field. She worked as a nurse for 33 years for the Los Angeles University of Southern California Medical Center.

After the 17th Street School was desegregated, the school pictures showed its growing diversity.

Her education led Mendez to a rewarding career. She also became a civil rights activist. She spoke out for equal treatment for all people regardless of their race. Although U.S. schools were desegregated after *Brown v. Board of Education*, racism remained a big problem in the country. In many places, it led to discrimination. This is when people are denied opportunities because of unfair reasons such as their race or gender. Racism and discrimination still exist today. But Mendez wants to help make sure that all children get the same educational opportunities.

Sylvia Mendez often gives speeches about racial equality, such as this one during Hispanic Heritage Month in 2014.

RISING TO THE TOP

During her time at the Los Angeles University of Southern California Medical Center, Mendez became the Assistant Nursing Director of the Pediatric Pavilion of the hospital.

This poster shows an enlarged version of the U.S. postal stamp that celebrates *Mendez v. Westminster*.

CHAPTER FIVE

5

REMEMBERING
THE PAST AND
CHANGING
THE FUTURE

Colonel Mark Toy honored Mendez with a Hispanic Heritage Month award in Los Angeles in 2011.

The *Brown v. Board of Education* case went down in history as a turning point in the fight against racial discrimination. But far fewer people know the story of Sylvia Mendez and her family's court battle. Even Mendez's younger sister, Sandra, did not know about it until she was in college. She came across the story one day in a book. She called her mother at once to ask her about it. Felicitas confirmed that it was their family's case.

CHAPTER **FIVE**

Sandra could not understand why no one had told her. Her mother explained that many people did not respond positively when the family had spoken of the victory. Some accused them of bragging. Others simply seemed uninterested. Eventually, her parents had decided to stop talking about it. Sandra saw what her mother meant when she brought the book to her professor. She told him that the story was about her family. But he barely acknowledged her. She was disappointed. She was proud of her sister and parents. She knew it was an important event in U.S. history.

Fortunately, many people want to remember and honor what Sylvia Mendez and her family accomplished in the fight against desegregation. One of those people is former President Barack Obama. In 2011, he awarded Mendez the Medal of Freedom for her dedication to equality in education. Following the ceremony, Mendez told the *Orange County Register*, "My parents just wanted what was best for their children. So, I have made it my life's work to spread their message."

President Obama places the Medal of Freedom around Mendez's neck during a ceremony at the White House in 2011.

Mendez is also proud of the difference she has made. But she worries that students are still getting separated by race. In 2014, UCLA's Civil Rights Project revealed that half of all Latino students in California attend schools in which 90 percent of the student body is Hispanic or African American. Many of these kids also live in poverty. In a 2017 interview with the *Daily Californian*, Mendez said, "If parents can't move out of ghettos and barrios, (their children) can't go to the white, 'good' schools."

Now in her 80s, Mendez is still touring the country through her activism work. She visits schools to teach young people about the importance of equality in education. She also tells them about her family's court case. Many of them have never heard of it. As she told *Teen Vogue*, "They often don't realize that the fight to receive a high-quality education and to keep discrimination out of schools is one that's been carried down by generations." She hopes that the kids she meets will keep fighting for this important right.

Sylvia Mendez has become an important activist in the
fight for equal education.

IN HONOR OF MENDEZ

In 2018, an elementary school in Berkeley, California was renamed Sylvia Mendez Elementary School to honor her work as an education activist.

1936   Sylvia Mendez is born in Santa Ana, California on June 7.

1946   The 17th Street School refuses to admit Sylvia Mendez because of her race.

Her family files a lawsuit against the Westminster, California school district to fight its whites-only policy.

U.S. District Court Judge Paul J. McCormick rules in favor of Mendez and the other families in the class action lawsuit.

1947   The U.S. Court of Appeals for the 9th Circuit upholds Judge McCormick's ruling.

California Governor Earl Warren signs a law, making school segregation illegal state-wide.

1948   Sylvia is finally admitted to the 17th Street School. Some of the white students bully her.

1954   *Brown v. Board of Education* makes segregation illegal in all U.S. schools.

2007   The U.S. Postal Service unveiled a stamp commemorating the *Mendez v. Westminster* case.

2011   President Barack Obama awards Mendez the Presidential Medal of Freedom.

2018   The Berkeley, California school renames an elementary school the Sylvia Mendez Elementary School to honor the education activist.

FIND OUT MORE

Conkling, Winifred. *Sylvia and Aki*. Berkeley, CA: Tricycle Press, 2013.

Mendez v. Westminster: Desegregating California's Schools. PBS. https://www.pbslearningmedia.org/resource/osi04.soc.ush.civil.mendez/mendez-v-westminster-desegregating-californias-schools/

Rubin, Susan Goldman. *Brown v. Board of Education: A Fight for Simple Justice*. New York: Holiday House, 2018.

Sylvia Mendez. SylviaMendezWestminster.com

http://sylviamendezinthemendezvswestminster.com/

Sylvia Mendez School. http://www.sylviamendezschool.org/who-is-sylvia-mendez

Tonatiuh, Duncan. *Separate Is Never Equal: Sylvia Mendez and her Family's Fight for Desegregation*. New York: Abrams Books for Young Readers, 2014.

WORKS CONSULTED

_____. "Background—*Mendez v. Westminster* Re-enactment." United States Courts. https://www.uscourts.gov/educational-resources/educational-activities/background-mendez-v-westminster-re-enactment

_____. "Health and Environmental Effects of Ozone Layer Depletion." United States Environmental Protection Agency. https://www.epa.gov/ozone-layer-protection/health-and-environmental-effects-ozone-layer-depletion

_____. "About Me." Sylvia Mendez. http://sylviamendezinthemendezvswestminster.com/contactus.html

_____. "Sylvia Mendez and Sandra Mendez Duran." StoryCorps. https://storycorps.org/stories/sylvia-mendez-and-sandra-mendez-duran/

Burress, Charles. "Emotion-filled Welcome for Sylvia Mendez at Sylvia Mendez School." Berkeley Public Schools, September 17, 2018. https://www,berkeleyschools.net/2018/09/emotion-filled-welcome-for-sylvia-mendez-at-sylvia-mendez-school/

Contreras, Daisy. "Sylvia Mendez: Pioneer in The School Desegregation Movement." NPR Illinois, September 18, 2017. https://www.nprillinois.org/post/sylvia-mendez-pioneer-school-desegregation-movement#stream/0

Jiménez, Jessíca. "Civil rights activist Sylvia Mendez speaks in Berkeley on integration." *The Daily Californian*, April 17, 2017. https://www.dailycal.org/2017/04/16/civil-rights-activist-sylvia-mendez-speaks-berkeley-integration/

Leal, Fermin. "O.C. civil rights icon Mendez awarded Medal of Freedom." *Orange County Register*, February 15, 2011. https://www.ocregister.com/2011/02/15/oc-civil-rights-icon-mendez-awarded-medal-of-freedom/

Meraji, Shereen Marisol. "Before 'Brown v. Board,' Mendez Fought California's Segregated Schools." NPR, May 16, 2014. https://www.nprillinois.org/post/brown-v-board-mendez-fought-californias-segregated-schools

Sarmiento, Isabella Gomez. "Sylvia Mendez Helped Integrate California Schools for Latinx Students in the 1940s, But She Says the U.S. Is More Segregated Now." *Teen Vogue*, December 3, 2018. https://www.teenvogue.com/story/sylvia-mendez-integrate-california-schools-latinx-students-1940s-more-segregated-now

Zonkel, Phillip. "Righting a wrong: *Mendez v. Westminster* brought an end to segregation in O.C. schools—and ultimately throughout the state and nation." Press Telegram. http://sylviamendezinthemendezvswestminster.com/aboutus.html

INDEX

ABOUT THE AUTHOR

Tammy Gagne has written more than 200 books for both adults and children. Among her favorites have been titles about people from different cultures with great passion for their life and work. Sylvia Mendez is one of these individuals. Others include Juan Felipe Herrera and Mario Molina. Gagne lives in northern New England with her husband, son, and a menagerie of pets.